Persephone's Husband:

Love Poems and Other Crimes

Amy Beth Katz

Living Dreams Press

Persephone's Husband © 2019 by Amy Beth Katz.
All rights reserved.

No part of this book may be used or reproduced in any manner whatsoever, including Internet, Ebook or audio recording, without written permission from *Living Dream Press* except in the case of brief quotations embodied in critical articles and reviews.

Living Dreams Press
1st Ed., First Printing, January 2, 2019.
Book design and cover photograph by Amy Beth Katz ©

Library of Congress Cataloging-in Publication Data
Katz, Amy Beth, 1968-
  Persephone's Husband: Love Poems and Other Crimes. — First ed.

ISBN-13: 978-1-943951-23-9 (Print Version)

Living Dreams Press
Santa Barbara, CA 93105
805-428-9252
www.livingdreamspress.com

Printed in the United States of America

To my Inner Companion,

With love

TABLE OF CONTENTS

The Systole Chapel   12
Ode to Pan   15
A Murder of Crows   20
The Heater   22
Cocooning   23
Lord of the Ring   25
Synesthesia of Love   27
Why I Want to Know Your Dreaming   31
Trust   34
I Am Monster   36
Lunch?   40
The Landscaper Commits Murder   43
Fortune   46
Cliff Hanger   47
The Things I am missing   48
Dive   51
Touch Screen   52
If Only In My Dreams   55
By My Side   57
Exile   59
The Substance of Melancholy   61
Trauma of Separation   62
Last Year's Leaves   64

You, Dark Wood   65
Sorrow   66
Discarded   67
Peeking   69
Kiss Me So We Know   70
Ecology 101   69
Bear Here   73
A Birthday Poem for Nils Peterson   75
Poems Are Like   77
Rocking the World   79
Medicine Walk with the Masked One   80
Something Other   86
Facebook Feed Poem (March 31, 2015)   89
Words Are Deviled Eggs   90
Captain Kirk Dream   92
When Herons Move as One   97
Photosynthesis: A Love Story, Part 1   100
Photosynthesis: A Love Story, Part 2   102
Angels on the Sand Ascending   104
My Mirror   106
Blind Star   108
Questions in the Forest   110
My Body is Braille   113

About the Author   116

"Out beyond ideas of wrong-doing
and right-doing,
there is a field.
I'll meet you there.

When the soul lies down in that grass,
the world is too full to talk about.
Ideas, language, even the phrase "each other"
doesn't make sense."
— *Rumi*

"Can We Talk?"

— Joan Rivers

THE SYSTOLE CHAPEL

Hades lives in my heart
deep in the left ventricle

I'll never have a coronary attack,
for he keeps the pulmonary unclogged
a painter keeping his tubes of oils
flowing
or a plumber

The corollary
is that at any moment he can reach up and grab me
by the throat and pull me down into my own beating
cavern
where persimmon blood splatters on the canvas
the Prince of Darkness peeling off layers
of an old fresco on an Italian wall
before beginning a new work

He likes to paint me naked
after I splunk into the bowels of the underworld
and frankly
I don't mind but sometimes it gets really cold and

dirty
and there is that relentless sound of a drum beating
and something running
through the rusted pipes
It puts me in a trance I can't seem to get out of
his glances up and down make my skin
flush pomegranate

This is the systole chapel
and Hades is none other
than Michelangelo
Scraping angels and diamons on my soul with his
scalpel and plaster
as pigeons in the belfry
flap their wings relentlessly
messengers of some archaic scribe
who lives in the brain

I wouldn't mind coming down now and then, but I
get trapped here all winter long
a Mother Bear in her cave of ice and snow.
Oh, she can come out, if the Dream Maker, Mr. Frost
or the Dark Artist will let her go

but they won't
You see,
it's a conspiracy of magnificent proportions

But Hades takes good care:
he covers me with a Grizzly rug
and bites my lip and tells me to sit still
as he puts the final touches on my
portrait,
then tosses it in the fire
and begins again
until Spring comes.
When he is finally done
he shows me the picture.
All I can see is a tree
with budding leaves made out of
arteries and acrylic
doves

He thinks I am pretty

I think Hell is paved
with Love

ODE TO PAN

What if Terror isn't something we ever "get over"?
What if Nightmare
isn't a bridge we cross
after paying the Trolls' toll
but is the cross?
The one we have to bare
—Sisyphus-style—
as we crucify ourselves on the trees of good and evil
and swallow our own serpentine tales?
The Ring of the Lords
is the Ouroboros.
It is cast of golden shadow.
Eve and Adam's wedding rings
slithered on their middle fingers.
Did you know they honey-mooned
at the forked tongue of the River Styx
which is always to be found at the mouth
of our own estuaries?

Nature never "gets over" her waterfalls and volcanoes

anymore than we overcome our hearts beating or
adrenaline crashing
on the cliffs of our brains or the wetness
between our legs.
Earthquakes are Gaia's shudderings and shivering;
typhoons her ecstasies and exhilarations,
geysers her ejaculations.
The Earth doesn't get over herself:
She whirls dervishly.
She accepts.
She surfs.
She sinks into cavernous holes of herself
and spews lava and fireballs
as she waits out eternity in sandstone and alligators
and blue whales
and calculates the sacred geometry of snails
and weighs the scales of red dragons
in their scientific lairs.
What if fear, if horror,
is something we cannot surpass
But at best, undress?

Pan lives in caves on cool hilltops
and beds down on damp forest floors.

He cannot resist a bonfire
or pulling down a zipper
and feeling for something warm and pulsing
inside.
He does this with lightening
speed and sharp fingernails
or very, very slowly, with his teeth.
The nymphs tell me
he is also pretty good with buttons,
undoing them...
pushing them...

Pan grows impatient
if the strip tease goes on too long:
he is always naked
and demands the same in us.
He plays at sado-masochism of the Soul
but this isn't a game, it's a rite.
There are no safe-words.
Pan is sure-footed on the ledges of our craggy fears.
He takes what he wants. He wants to give.
He speaks in thrusts and tongues
even as he licks our ears and when
we offer our jugular to him;

when we surrender on our backs and stretch our necks
and offer blood as if to fangs of vampire;
when we feel the truth raging in our veins
that we share his pulse and chloroform,
he feels green and hard and heard.

Then, and only then,
will he hold his reed flute erect,
—All beast, all man—
and exhale raindrops and butterflies,
blades of grass and bucking stags,
daffodils, ancient oaks and thorns of rose
so that we can inhale his fresh mountain air.

When we breath together this way—
the Horned God's tongue filling up our mouths,
the human moans echoing in the canyon of his throat—
the heavens and the earth harmonize in pitchfork perfect union.
Only then does enemy become ally;
war story transcends into epic poem;
a fallen angel re-pairs his mossy wings.

And the cross?
The cross spreads her loving arms
and lets Ecstasy and Terror
hug her close.

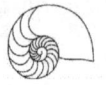

A MURDER OF CROWS

I've been noticing of late
how often I hop or rush away abruptly
from the ones I want to stay with
most

Bunnies behave this way
So do swallows, hummingbirds,
hours in old age; water
falls
the brave and timid ones
afraid of our own
shadows and wolves
in sheep's lingerie

It's what is underneath the soft wool
that frightens us the most

Crows are different, though
They claim a branch, a sign post
or bust of Pallas and hold
their ground emboldened
by the unexpected Presence

of what they crave the most:
a round-table feast
a gesture just for them or telling of a dream
enchantment in the wild forest
trust

Sometimes they will even
take one step closer
and reveal ruffled feathers
which long for preening
touch
by bird or hand or prophetic
message from the dead, or gone

The closeness of such wild beauty
keeps stunning us awake
while lips parted
never cease whispering
us whole

THE HEATER

I saw you
leaning up against the heater
lofty, brooding
adrift on a raft no one else could see
melancholy dripping from the fibers of your being
as if you had fallen overboard in salty sea
or been sitting in the bathtub fully clothed until the water ran cold.

I knew, even then that I loved you.

Many years later,
I saw that same look of devastated
longing on your face
As I passed you by in the courtyard and suddenly
I knew myself better
than I ever had before.

COCOONING

I hear the beating of wings of doves
outside the window
the cry of hummingbirds for the sugar
you will give to them this day
and a sentry crow announcing the coming
of an August storm, or my wishful thinking of one

I run the fingers of my imagination
through the soft bird-down of your temple
and kiss your still sleeping mouth. A silver
trout stirs the surface of the water
the lake trembles under the weight of a dragon-
fly's shadow
you wake to feel my hand on your body through
your lavender sheet of dreams
my palm
trees swaying
feeling your sun and your heart
drumming a little faster now as darkness slips away
and my hips become a magnet for rhythm
and moss

I breathe you into me
as deep as the forest in a faery
tale breathes in the dawning of a new
story I breath in your eucalyptus
your cascading
fountains as the butterfly of my soul
alights on the red rose of yours,
and is invited in

We cocoon in our awakening

LORD OF THE RING

"How are you doing?" You asked me,
as we were sitting in front of every one.
"Good!" I said, pleased with myself.
"Usually I fall madly in love with men like you."
"How am I doing?" You asked me, wryly; amused.
"So far, so good! I don't feel anything….because I
noticed that ring on your finger.
Now, if that weren't there,
that would be another story, entirely."

"Hmmmm…" you said, slightly bruised.

I thought that declaration
would makes us both bullet proof—
You seemed to take it as a challenge;
Or, I hoped you would.

I should have known better. I should
have brought an armored tank with me
whenever I was in your presence
Or Gandalf.

He would have known what a Hobbit like me
should do with one such as you.
Or am I smeagol?
God, how I hate that ring! (And covet it too.)
You still wear it around your finger

But every time I hug you, or imagine
I do
I feel it as a noose around my neck,
like Frodo,
on his way to Mount
Doom.

SYNESTHESIA OF LOVE

We're endless miles away
yet I can feel your heart pulsing next to mine,
your body radiating light in the darkness
of 5 A.M. on a wintery day.
What if the whole world can feel us too?

Maybe this is what they mean by "angels":

A man with synesthesia passes by my glowing window, is is overcome by grace, and glimpses wings.

A teen-age girl,
midway between your neighborhood and mine
Half-way between childhood and motherhood
begins trembling unexplainably like the autumn
leaves of the Apple Tree, upon whose lap she dwells.
Too young to know the ways of the world,
Her body says a miracle is taking place.
She grows up to be an Arborist.
She gives birth to seventeen children.

In the darkening temple of our imagination
my fingertips stroke the swanny down along your temple
and in the church at the end of your street,
a juvenile delinquent dragged there by his Mother,
makes fun of the Virgin Mary.
An unlit prayer candle on her alter spontaneously
resurrects, exploding into flame.
In awe and the good kind of shame
a voice within him vows he will become a priest one day.
He does.
He conducts a boys choir. He leads vespers.
He leaves the church at midlife and becomes a Buddhist. He beds a beauty named Mary who told him she can't get pregnant. Every Christmas, he builds a nativity scene in the barn for his son,
who they named Jesus.

In the stillness just before birdsong,
our tongues flutter out of the rafters
our legs and arms snake from underneath the porch
we burrow into the nest we make together
half way across town, across the universe.

We earth-quake.

Somewhere towards the North, a Glacier calves.
And in the East, the sun rises over golden waves
upon which the fishermen on a sailing vessel,
lost at sea, think they spot an Albatross and blink
back tears, in unison. They cheer with hope.
But not the Captain, that old, embittered mariner,
who has been frowning into the swirling water for
days, for years, he swears he finally sees the lovely
mermaid,
beckoning him to join her.
Nobody sees him climbing overboard.
Nobody sees him ever again.
Nobody misses him.
But the siren sings her sweetest, salty songs to him,
and in the muffled deeps his voice melts into hers:
he feels true love for the first time in his 69 years.

And as he drowns in her embrace;
as their wedding song deepens into a whale's dirge
we hear them moaning through our gills and throats
and we feel their quivering in our one, arching, mer-
maid spine.

Our bones fuse, and sing.
The sound smells like roses.

WHY I WANT TO KNOW YOUR DREAMING

Why I want to know your dreaming is why
I want to touch the silky scaled wing
of butterfly

and know the softness and the shape
of grace
from the inside out
and hold your fluttering in my heart
for just a moment, or forever
whichever lasts longer
and discover what it is to fly, or land,
or sink or die from your particular cocoon,
or rose, or grave.

The common fear (and fear is so common)
is that after one touches a butterfly's wing
the oil from our hands will contaminate
or weigh it down, and make us executioner.
It is true
we must respect the faery powder that gives her
flight.
But Peter Pan tickled Tinkerbell

and this only made her fly higher,

and sometimes landings are in order,
and maybe even executions.

I do not want to pin your wings down like a science
project or taint the floating parchment for arts'
sake or keep you in a looking-glass
cage.
I want simply want to taste the sweetness
and the bitterness at the mouth of your blossoming
and land solidly in the middle of the parting
of your red seas
and know the seeing of your big dark eyes
and to feel the feeling that vibrates out of your huge
antenna;
to learn the secrets of the turning and the tuning
and the craving of moths burning
in the sacred flames profane with Eros
and to fly away fly away fly away into the baby blue
transformed and transforming
stagnant waters into blood red wine
thirsty still thirsty still for all the nectar
you and I have yet to swallow

at the top of a spiraling tower
under a young Moon.

This is why I want to enter chrysalis, together
And fall asleep in our Acsclepian caves of make-be-
lieves
and weep and hope impatiently
patient
for the great demise
of Caterpillar,

and maybe, may be even butterfly
so we can reincarnate
into dream.

TRUST

I am shy, I know.
I need to learn many things.
I am a feral cat longing for warmth of hearth and home but still
living close to the memory of cold streets and darkness.

This world is new to me
and I sense you have leapt off the edge too, and are suspended in mid-air.
But I do know how to scoop up a drowning bee
out of the deep end and dry off its wings
after he has fallen off the breeze's trapeze.
And I am willing to get stung
if that's what it takes to ensure the pro-creation
of honey, the health of the hive
and the sanctity of the Queen.

I have no intention of stinging you!

But in the back alleyways and brackish
swamplands of the past, I have felt the scalpel fangs
of Nature
with my own tongue, and known the hunger of the
stray and the wild cat;
I apollogize in advance for when I do,
(sting you)
and will do all to rebuild our safe nest
when I fly back to the highest branches of our Self.

We all have syringes like the snake
that taste of bitter medicine.
But I get the importance of good measurement
and the commitment to the administration of ongo-
ing doses, and patience.
The patience of pines, furs, redwoods, oaks
turtles, tarantulas and tree frogs,
frozen in ice.

I have taken the Aesclepian Oath
and swallowed it whole.

I am placing this carnelian serpent on my finger
as a wedding ring, next to the mortal, golden one.

Together they form an infinity
sign.
As we wait to thaw
I will not forsake us.

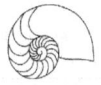

I AM MONSTER

I am the monster
on the other side
of the door
that has always been
In the center of the room.
It figures
as my invisibility wears off
you saw me reaching out with my Komodo dragon
claws
grasping at air, as you shivered under your chair.
I have not been understanding
that what looks to me like a Princess's dainty hands
are really fingers covered in porcupine quills and
daggers.
I thought I couldn't sew, or rent
but now I see I could tear the fabric of your world
apart
with one stroke of my finger, whether it's coaxing,
pointing, wagging, or standing upright like a soldier.
An innocent child looks out of the mirror at me,
but what you see in my reflection is a devil older
than time

madly grinning. You smile back,
when you aren't running away for your life.
My courtly robes are stately; graceful,
but look again and you will see they are really tattered shreds of fabrications
of who I wanted to believe I was.
This giant toad body is oozing slime
Great gobs puddling green and mud
On the threshing floor;
You are here with me
All of you
But it's been so dark
The vessel was ill-formed and I, uninformed.
How can it be when the void keeps shifting shape
like a ghost-orb caught on camera
or an embryo, or the arteries of your terrified heart?
And you've been holding your breath all this time
One ear to the door,
As your worst fears and greatest longings loomed
behind you, casting giant shadows in the shape
of me.
Only when you "make the stop" as we do with
nightmares
does Banshee's wail

recede inward Into
silence.
Only when you cast your magic eyes upon me
does my ugliness turn to beauty.
Only now
Can I begin to hear the throb of your own
Monstrous orb, and see the fur and scales
covering your own nakedness.
Only now in the seeing of our true natures
is it safe
to touch
Monster skin against Monster skin
we glow green in the Erie light;
our roars in each other's throats
turning into
purrs.

LUNCH?

If you met me for lunch
we would want to impress each other.

My lipstick would be on straight
glowing pink as bubble gum, or cherry
pie. You'd be
hungry and wearing my favorite color
and be smelling real nice and we would be shy to-
gether so my hands might shake
and in an attempted display of perfect, high-cultured
manners
I'd drop my lettuce on the table or knock over my
Artisan Spring Water
onto your lap but I couldn't dare dapple it up with
my napkin because I would want to touch you too
much and thus would not get too close so you might

shiver a little from the ice
but by the time our main course came you will have
made me laugh or cry and that will warm us up

although I will have a billion things to share with you
and thus might not be able to speak at all and so you
will have to do all the talking or maybe
we would say nothing at all (like the song)

and maybe we would speak only through the tin-
kling of glasses and fork tines tapping china
and your fingers flying through air and your stag-eyes
making love to the dear of mine.

Maybe it won't be until sometime after that you will
kiss me and break the evil spell, and then I would
talk your ear off for the rest of the meal, or eternity
and then you would have to kiss me again to keep
me quiet in this and all our future lives together.
(To keep me really silent you would have to use your
tongue,
but that would only make me moan louder and
louder so there isn't much hope of living in peace
from now on or eternity
IF we were to go on a date.)

When we meet for our first lunch-date,

I will want to eat something chocolate for dessert or maybe warm blueberry pie with my red wine or cappuccino or anything decadent because that is the feeling of how you feed my soul with your words and gestures and I know I will be so jeoulous of the glass in your hand, how lucky is the rim! And especially, your spoon,

how you make her shine!
I'll long to be your napkin, too, but will settle for the time being with being your butter-knife
until I move up in your world (or down).

Unless you don't like me in which case I would become your steak-knife
Then I would feel really sad and just wish that I was your filet minion and while I lasted I had tasted better.
No, I might be too afraid of you calling the waiter over and sending me back to the kitchen to ever go on a lunch-date with you...
(although, I am free for dinner...)

How about you?

THE LANDSCAPER COMMITS MURDER

The Landscaper rides by on the grinding machine so loud
I fear I will not hear Ziona's dream over Skype.
He tries to mow down the tall grass and violet wildflowers, ones the rain gods and I took three months to grow from dust.
Someone in me stands guard, prepared to throw the four pointed Chinese star of myself
in front of the rapacious blades.
"The boss of the corporation told me to cut down everything"
he says, in broken English.
The bosses always do.

I gesture in broken Earthling, "not these: not these! They are beautiful."
The flowers quiver. The green weeps. The landscaper frowns.
He proceeds in chopping down everything else
but the thin smile of earth at the edge of my dream council,
which in the end looks like a jack-o-lanterns grin,

ridiculous slice of a crop circle
surrounded by the buzz cut of Aphrodite's hair a
block wide
no longer silky and sensuous, blowing in the breeze,
now she looks like an ascetic monk, a military cadet,
or cancer victim after chemo.

I wonder for a moment at my determined resolve:
should I have given in? Will this get us kicked out of
the campground?
I look at the waves of wild grasses on the nearby hill-
sides,
and the vast forest beyond, which is just a minute's
walk away.
Did I need to save the wildness all the way up to my
doorstep?
The Sun Goddess wails for the lost snails and sweet
blades of Olympus and Pan, who is still green
but now only one inch tall
cannot hear the sound of his own flute
as the annoyed Gardner silently curses me
as he continues riding the killing machine.
Thor runs across the rainbow bridge
I shake his hammer at the depravity of civility

and drop down to my knees
in supplication to the death row of wildflowers
known only to the executioners as weeds.
Yes! Gaia screams. Yes!

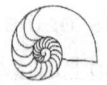

FORTUNE

You are not a God.
You are not even the Devil.
You are a just a dude in a funny hat
wearing Hawaiian shorts.
I am not a Goddess.
I am not a Lion or a Witch.
I am just a Fool in love who has nothing left
to wear, or lose,
but still wants to walk through the Wardrobe
and inhabit
you.
If I had a crystal ball that could foretell the future,
I would throw it at you!

I wonder, would you see it
coming?

CLIFF HANGER

Don't fall
over
the cliff.
Fall with
the cliff
over
your old
self.

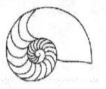

THE THINGS I AM MISSING

The Things I am Missing

I am missing looking into your eyes
and seeing what color they tint
with each of your moods;
knowing when I please you,
or exasperate you, or delight you.
I am missing knowing what it is
to hear you talk about your day:
the little things: what someone said that struck you
like lightening or a fist or a
revelation.
When you pray, what God's name do you whisper?
What do you like to order
in a restaurant?
What amuses you in each moment?
Do you think I am pretty?
Will you blush if I compliment you?
Will you be seduced with a glance,
or a hand on your thigh under the table?
Where at the table do you like to sit?
What is the shape

of your kiss?
If my lips could linger at your throat,
or that depression between your neck and collar
bone, would that make you happy?

What one caress or lick would turn all your lights
on? Is anybody home?
Do you laugh when you make love?
Do you cry, or moan?
Do you cuddle after?
Do you like to fall asleep curled in your lover's arms?
Do you prefer to sleep alone?
Do you like to brush your teeth in the morning before your woman makes love to you again, or no?
Do you mind staying up all night?
Do you want to watch the sun rise with me over the warm ocean waters, and bathe in the wild river?
Do you fish?
Do you like your lover to hug you at random times?
To stop whatever she is doing and tell you how much you mean to her?
Do you like her to sing to you, or whisper in your ear what she is going to do to you before she does it?
Do you like to be the one to seduce her?

What are your techniques?
Do you listen as well with your body to hers as you
do with your ears?
Do you ever dream of going somewhere
you have never been before, and if so, where?
Would you like someone who would go anywhere
you wanted any time, with you,
and was ecstatic just to be with you?
Do you like it when a woman confronts you and tells
you when you are being a jerk?
When you are with your true love,
are you always good to her?

Can I be your true love?

DIVE

Every time the surf laps over the seashore
and the waves kiss the land
the Earth moans a little, and trembles,
shifting the sands.

Do you feel it?
Do you hear it?
Step outside if you don't,
and breathe.

Your breathing is the inhale and the exhale
of the tides,

Your sighs
the ancient comminglings of water
and gravity
dive for me
for the secrets buried
in the below the wake

TOUCH SCREEN

I wish I were the Touch Screen
on your Iphone.

I wish I were the sea shell
you bring up to your ear,
and your microphone.

I wish I were the hand you use to recite
the Pledge of Allegiance,
and the finger you say "Shhhhhhhhhh" with.

I wish I were your tie,
the foam in your Cappuccino,
your spoon.

I wish I was the pillow you will hug tonight
and the sheet that gets tangled around your legs
in your restless slumber,
and the dream in which you become
lucid.
I wish I were your lucidity.

I wish I were the sunrise that greets you in the morning, and the birdsong; the arm
you cover your eyes with to fall back to sleep until noon,
I wish I were the sand behind your knees,
the little spot of shaving cream you missed,
the mud oh-so-gently sucking your toes.

I wish I were the hot August sun on your back
on a three Margarita afternoon;
both your hat and the wind, stroking your hair.
I wish I were your Chapstick,
your suntan oil applied slowly at the lake,
your wallet in your back pocket (or the front),
your Cuban cigar
and your 50 year-old Scotch sipped
all evening long.

I wish I were the floor where you kneel down
to pray,
the snow where you make angels,
the green grass under your belly
and the Oak tree that hugs you from behind
when you lean your back up against it

for support.

I wish I was the air you breathe,
the water in which you swim
Your campfire on the beach,
your hallowed ground.

I wish I were your fragrant rose,
the sheath of your sword,
and the vessel of your Soul.

I wish I were your Djembe drum,
your rattle-goard,
your thimble and your rule
of Thumb.

I wish I were your angel wings.
I wish I were your crown of thorns.
I wish I was your Teddy Bear or if you lost it long ago
I wish I were the finding of your childhood
dreams.

IF ONLY IN MY DREAMS

Sometimes I don't know if I am talking with God,
the Man upstairs,
or the Black Madonna in high heals.
It is true I have fallen
in love with my Self.
Alone, I am Trinity.

Yet that is no less devastating
then falling for a man on a cross,
a rock star,
or one with a boulder
on his finger.
One would think, "at least she is always there for herself."

To that, I reply,

> "Shooting stars fall, too.
> Dolphins get lost in the storm.
> Worms wiggle out of soil in the rain
> and if they get stepped on,
> they may be cut in half.

> Then they have to find their selves all over again,
>
> Like a shoe lost at sea.
>
> The Ferris Wheel turns at top of every new year,
> And put's it foot down now and then.
> The Roller Coast screams
> and puts it's hands up in the air."

Is it rising to the occasion and having fun,
or terrified, deep down?

Fear of losing oneself is reflective
of losing the love of others.

That's why I pray to the mirror every night, now.
And long for it to sing back three-fold prayers.

If only
in my dreams.

BY MY SIDE

I so hope someday,
I will find the man who can stand to stand not in
front of me,
or in back of me,
or off to the side;
not only have me waiting in the wings for him, but
be, truly, by my side, center stage.
A man who is so fiercely proud of me,
He is willing to say to the world,
"She is my friend.
I will never let anyone hurt her
or be unkind to her again,
as long as I am alive!
I will shield her with my grace."

I so hope one day soon this man will walk up to me
and put his arms around me
and in no uncertain terms say, "I love you."
The last puzzle piece on the story's face.
A man who does anything
he can to be close, and show his adoration.

A man who says, "There will always be a seat reserved for you
in the temple
of my heart, and my hearth.
I want you close to me,
inside and outside."
A man who not only gives me a place at the table,
who clears one for me so I may take my own,
but one who pulls the chair out for me, next to him,
pours the wine, and welcomes me.
A man whose whole life is our embrace.

For, this is the man who knows that if he ever needs to know how loved he is,
if he ever needs to know the shape of his own heart;
all he ever has to do is look deeply
into my eyes, or kiss my lips:
to eat from my banquet;
to affirm his own "yes" in the mirror
of my acceptance
and to listen to my soul
singing endlessly to him.

EXILE

When they told me today,
"relinquish hope for tomorrow,
due to yesterday's demons"
What could I have said?
I cannot speak, to explain.

There are no words for sunrises in the desert.
There are no words for flocks of pelicans soaring
against an azure sky;
There are no words for rainbows at the golden hour,
or moonlight dancing on the lap of evening's black-
ening water.
There are no words for the words we never speak
to each other,
the volumes that only our hearts have read.

If I were a tree, all my leaves would have fallen
In that moment of no-hope.
Once again,
I am a bare sapling shivering
in the shadow of the ax of fear.
The stars are still here burnishing and branding

the heavens;
cookie cutter stars shaped like Christmas,

But you took the ladder away.
I cannot breath the scent of ginger and goodness,
or taste the sweetness.
So I don't want to breath.
I would rather draw water into my lungs
then be separated from the flame of my desire.
I would rather be exhiled on the moon
then be alone here on Earth
separated from her Aesclepian Sun.
I would rather go hungry to bed,
or to the grave,
then live without the source of all healing:
To live without hope.

THE SUBSTANCE OF MELANCHOLY

The water drips from the faucet
that won't turn off.
It is the drip drip drip of the clock ticking,
my heart beating monotonously
my soul bleeding out of my blue eyes
into an aquamarine pool that forms on the counter
and drips drips drips onto the rosewood floor.
The clouds are white, and the gold sun shines on the
highest peak in the last light of the day, but my eyes
are grey.
There is no distinction between day and night,
only night hides the dark circles.
At night, no one can see the spirals downward.
No one can see the stairs that lead to Hell's sitting
room
or Persephone's husband waiting for me
there.

TRAUMA OF SEPARATION

Walking down State Street
in a dissociative trance-state
limbs slow and aching
walking through quick sand in a dream
it takes all her effort to move forward
she is shattering into a thousand pieces
she is coming undone, unglued, unhinged
too many layers that contrast each other
too many lies and truths all at once
her heart feels like it it has stopped
she fears she really cannot breath
menstrual cramps begin
her heart is bleeding
her hands are trembling
she shivers in the August heat
marrow of her bones is cold
she begins to faint
she catches herself
Does he hate me this much?
Does he love me this much?
Does he mean never to see me again?
Does he mean to find me in some way?

IS he only ever going to destroy me?
IS he ever going to help me be who I can be?
Is he hurting this much, too?
Does he know something I don't know?
Why won't he speak to me?
Is this what it is going to be always?
Is he acting out of fear or bravery?
Is he a sadist or a saint?
How will we ever be together again?

LAST YEAR'S LEAVES

I'll just fade away
like a dream or a leaf
it was beautiful in all its colors
everyone marveled at the life-fire,
the veins, the shape.
Then, as if without warning, it turned brown and molted
and people began stepping on it,
mistaking it for dirt,
as if it is alright to walk on the earth
without noticing.
Some things are camouflaged in life,
other's in death,
and I?
I am the mat at the doorway in between
and under that,
the dusty threshing floor,
scattered with last year's
leaves.

YOU, DARK WOOD

I am lost, in these dark woods of you.
I do not know what hides under the shade of your
mushrooms and your thickets
of blackberry brambles.
I do not know your intentions or the whys of your
curling tendrils and vines-
Do they reach for me? Or only for you to grow closer
to yourself?

I am lost in the forbiddenness.
In time that is biding;
In the bid-thee-well-ness
Of your wishing well.
Would you have me drown here
If drowning means eternal yearning?
Or will you pull me up in a bucket, hand-over-hand
And bring me to your unquenchable mouth and
drink me
until I am full?

I am lost somewhere between this thirst and this
over-flowing;
between your reflection and the face of love itself.

I am lost between the certainty of our tangled roots
and the confusion of the budding
shoots of not-knowing.
I am lost between the yearning and the satisfaction
And sometimes even in the finding.
I am lost somewhere between the dying-leaf floor of
your silence
And the green canopy of your abundant offering.
I am lost in these dark woods of you.

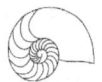

SORROW

Yesterday I was smiling.
So was the Sun high above the Thunderclouds.
We've been praying for rain all winter long
Who knew the safety of the drought
Would end like this: the Sky opening up
A teen age girls knees spreading on the horizon.
This is how the innocent navigate toward's Earth's
Abyss.
And how the guilty try avoiding cliffs but fall anyway,
Brown leaves scattering into mulchy grave.

Gravity stomps to the bar and orders a cognac or a
Guinness,
and I slip to the bottom of the quick sand
sinking,
sinking fast.
I might come
out the other end of the world at the end
of a century or in China,
or some other drunken God's bed but
all I want is to be in yours
alone. alone.

DISCARDED

Maybe it is better to "fade away
into obscurity"
to be a crimson leaf returned to brown
earth
a broken shell or
snakeskin floating
on wind

Today I am the salt of tear drop
an elephant tusk
the silky husk of corn

PEEKING

Peeking on Facebook;
seeing what is underneath
the surface of things on the
news.
Dervishes dancing entranced as I lay with the Mystery of it all
hanging over my head like Mistletoe,
or a noose.

KISS ME SO WE KNOW

I feel like such a Fool today.
Why is it foolish to express love?
Rumi did it, and a hundred million dervishes
whirl in a hundred million hearts each time they
read his Poetry.
Christ did it, and two thousand years later
a billion Believers across the planet still feel it.
The trees do it,
every Spring when their buds open green
in honor of the sun.

Today, I am a fool and tomorrow,
if you catch me being anything else, run!

Or perhaps, fling your arms around my neck
And kiss me so we know
Fools are in good company
And we are not alone.

ECOLOGY 101

I'd probably get a "D" on a biology test
but I know how to feel into the heart of a lion
and how to shed skin while moving in
the body of a snake.

I have discovered that the hair closest to the pores
of a wild boar feels softest
and that the fetus of a Kangaroo crawls
out of her mama's womb and into her pouch
weeks before she is ready to give birth
to the World.

I might forget the names of things geological
but I can tell you where all the black bear trails are
and where the bobcat crosses Paradise Road
and what time is the Golden Hour
at any given place on Earth.

I am not an Ornithologist
but I have seen where the hummingbirds sleep
and have even held the fluttering of a ruby-throated
in my hand;

I was surprised the sword of her beak
did not hurt
and that her heart beat
louder than mine.

I am not a zoologist or a priest,
but I can teach you how to call predators to you
by offering yourself as pray.
To follow the animals to their dens
and listen in so deeply you might breath
in unison with the mountain lion
and fall asleep to her purring.
(I am not an ophthalmologist
but I did this on a vision quest.)

Now I am learning how to be on a vision quest every day
and still do the wash and clean the house
How to spirit-track a mouse
when taking out the garbage;
and ride on the wake of blue whales
on the way to Science class.

BEAR HERE

There is something about the crackling
of branches, the sway of green, the parting
of the grasses; the two dark triangles of ears
poking up from the sea of Devil's Club
like miniature shark fins synchronized in swim.
When she sashays onto the path, her black
eyes meet mine, blue; the bruise between us heals.
Lightening strikes itself. In between the push and pull
of fear and love, from the den emerges hope.
She's only going about her day, like us.
I wonder if the chalky sound of shoes on rocks
and the danger of our vicious possibilities
thrills her into awareness, too?
We only worship light because it leans
up against the darkness.
We only cherish life when death is panting
and rubbing up against our trembling legs.
We only belly laugh when the relief
that nothing worse can happen rises up
as phoenix from the ashes of our grief
into the revelation that we stalk the beast
even as he stalks us.

Do bears chuckle like people and parrots?
I have heard them cry
when they think no one else is listening.

A BIRTHDAY POEM FOR NILS PETERSON:

Sometimes moles are not moles at all
but wild stallions or tulip bulbs
or vulnerable dragons
in autumn's lair.

Sometimes moles are exactly what moles are
and the black, moist soil of a gardner's garden smiles
and says, snuggle in closer!
And if worms could talk
they would croon to mole in earthy verse,
and the bedrock would soften and give way
(only to him!)
and the Mysteries sleeping underneath
would welcome him into her deeps.

Sometimes moles are and are not what they are.
When that is so, the earth that holds
quakes;
Crimson possibilities flow from volcanos
and burrowing mammals rise into mountain peeks.

This is how the moon can kiss moles cheek.

This is how stretching sun can give him
a birthday hug
and stars can tuck him in after cake and candles
to dreamy sleep.

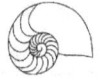

POEMS ARE LIKE

Poems are like
hot chocolate
hugs, puppies
swimming laps
pirate maps
umbrellas
new shoes still
in the box
Diplomas
scissors, sharp
barber shop
quartets. Stop

signs poems are
home-made soup
cans of beans
leaning tow-
ers, sausage
pizza, France

the color
green poems
are frogs blue

sky, moon's
eye the kiss
I promise

poems are like
you and I
in every
thing we do

Poems are like
Vanilla
Ice cream on
Silver spoons.

ROCKING THE WORLD

I'll never be as good as you
I'll never be hero, saint or nun
or robin who earns the early worm
I'll always run, a little
hot and cold
with lead seeping slowly from my pipes
even as the crystal mountain waters flow
through my mouth
I will always be more bedrock than gold
more fire in the veins than blood
more Twin
Towers crashing and crumbling down
than rising sun
But when dust clouds blot out the day
and acid rain falls
when Isis turns from goddess to banshee
and God plays with his nuclear toys once more
I will be umbrella to your worries
Persephone to your Hades
I will be down below or up-above for you, always
rocking the world in my arms

MEDICINE WALK WITH THE MASKED ONE

I am sitting outside in my front yard,
waiting for a client, who doesn't show up.
The red candle is flickering; the sweet grass drifting
through the warm air, the tea bubbling in the Japanese tea pot.
I look at the two little cups,
and the stunning mountains in the distance,
and consider calling a friend to share the beauty.
But a voice says,

"Be still... wait and see who comes to you."

I sip from one cup, and then slowly,
begin to drink from the other...

As I do, a bell chimes, announcing an e-mail has arrived: curious timing. I open it.
It is a message from our "Advanced Dreamtending" mentor, further instructing, "Follow your curiosity..."

My thoughts flirt with the things I have been most
curious about this week:
a pomegranate sliced open, and bleeding:
too bitter to put into my smoothy
(or so I think: later I am to learn bitterness is medi-
cine.)
The fruit bleeds all over my cutting board and the
crimson juice looked so lovely, I leave it out for two
days on the counter and then dip a paint brush in it
to create abstract art, in honor of Persephone, God-
dess of the Underworld.
I have also been curious about a rainbow that ap-
peared, out of the blue, outside my window, which
had begged me to go outside and photograph it.
That's when I had noticed the grassy area and woods
beyond, across the road,
that I had yet to explore, which could be a place to
hold a dream council...

Now, back in the moment, that unexplored terrain
grabs ahold of my curiosity again, and I can not re-
sist. I almost run across the gully; a deep recess in
the Earth. I am wearing a skirt and the grass is knee-

high: I slow down and exercise caution, as I follow snake trails and mountain lion sign. The animal trails

lead me deeper into the thicket, where I stumble upon three old, dilapidated tin and chicken wire structures.

I become aware that now I am much closer to the Indian Burial grounds, and the dark presences there awaken.

"Time to go!" the fearful little girl within me shouts. But then, a most shocking revelation blossoms like a time-lapsed rose: "I must return here soon, with the "Masked One": the one who waits beyond the locked doors, from my eternity of nightmares: only he can face what is out in THESE woods.

I realize that the dreamwork I have done with my new friends the day before has prepared me for this...
not knowing what "this" was.
That's when I am shown a single, exotic and ancient sage plant, growing among the brambles and thorny

weeds. I carefully pick a handful, understanding perfectly what it is to be used for, and what it is not. (Even though my conscious mind is still in the dark.)

This is where my curiosity leads me. But, this was only the beginning. It is contagious. For just tonight, after the rains, a fading love asks if we might walk back out to the place I had told him about, "the mysterious place, with the ancient structures". So we head out, this time, in the dark. As I slip on my rubber boots and leave the familiarity of the road for the wilds, fear rises up in me. I ask the "Masked One" from my nightmare to be my protector, and he shows up immediately. (I am very surprised I wasn't scared of him. But there was much more to be scared of in this black forest woods, I suppose.) I ask my friend whom he wants to call forth as a protector, to accompany us from the Dreamtime. "Mickey Mouse" he says. I sigh... he doesn't take the Dreamtime so seriously. But then, I smile: he is here with me, isn't he? And so is Mickey Mouse! Just the levity both of us need to feel safe in the dark.

Just when we reached the old structures of tin and barbed wire, I feel a new presence behind us, watching us, and spin around.

A Deer!

So this is where my curiosity, and the Masked One leads!

A week or so later, I am at the Chumash Casino, Watching my boyfriend play a slot machine. Suddenly, I am aware of the Masked One. His presence is here with me! Only he has shape-shifted into a Kabuki Samurai. My friend continues pressing buttons, winning bonuses. I look at the figure in my mind's eye: he is leaning up against the Zorro Machine. His skin glistens as with suntan oil; His arm are strong, his eyes deep brown. I feel him put his arms around me, and hold me tight. I feel my physical body responding to the imaginary presence. I am aware how different he feels than the flesh and blood man sitting in front of me. I feel a flush of guilt, that releases into the air like smoke, and is gone. He's only imaginary!

And yet, I have fallen deeply in love with him.

A short while later, I wander around to another bank of machines, and I am shocked at what I see: a Kabuki Samurai themed slot machine. I put in a $20, and hit the jackpot.

SOMETHING OTHER

I should write poems about something other than
love and desire.

Don't you think?

The bees are getting weary and need to sleep.
The butterflies are dying and Spring
is no where in our sights.
The rams parts go unwatched
fireworks fizzle out before they stream
Pan's flute is broken and the silver trout are full of
doubt.
The thin-skinned frogs are indicator species, but not
a single one sees any sign of a golden ball. The frogs
wear sweats instead of Victoria's Secret lingerie.
The Princess is a lesbian. No, scratch that. A nun.
My pen is impotent: it might as well be a limp carrot
before a non-existent horse.
The cart does not put out.

I could write instead about practical matters. About
drinking sugared coffee at 12:00 am.

The laundry piled up that never ends: it's caught in
its own obsession with the washer and dryer, a dirty,
polygamous affair,
but I've sworn not to tell.
I could write about bird cages waiting to be cleaned:
used newspaper, out-dated,
waiting to be replaced.
I could write about the absence or clear-cutting of
trees, and describe the styrofoam to-go-box whose
inner sides are red with impassioned spaghetti wait-
ing to fling its body into the bed of the recyclables,
foreplay
to global warming.
(There I go again!)
Maybe best to stick to the election woes:
nothing sexy there.

But where does this abstinent imagery get us?
Feeling empty and slow.
There is a lump of coal in my Christmas stocking.
Tonight I will likely have a nightmare, of nothing.

On second thought,

maybe I should stick to love and desire?

There is nothing very good about
this poem.
It's a bra with no underwire.
It is ritual without alter;
warm keg beer, when we could be drinking exquisite
sentences of Brute champagne and eating clauses of
caviar from a hot bubble bath of sonnets.
After all, we could be speaking
in tongues.
Yes.
Let's!

FACEBOOK FEED POEM (MARCH 31, 2015)

Thitch Nat Han, in red monk robe
and eyes looking inward holds a flower,
"True love is offering peace and happiness to another."
The Opossum mother and her 8 babies on the road of life
Brings us to our Knees; to mercy.
"Hanukkah, 5692, 'Judea dies'", thus says the Nazi Banner.
 8 Hanukkah lights in an east coast apartment across from it retort,
 "Judea lives forever".
Travel isn't a hobby, it's a sport. Follow us!
Santa Monica Pier, the place of movies and nostalgia
Momma cuddles a kitty.
A Republicans phone keeps moronically autocorrecting "Obama to Moron".
Some river time after mountain skiing makes for a good day.
Flowers in bloom
people watching at the airport

A real conversation is sexy
Thanks for the music!

Smiling family at the waters edge:
the dawn of expressionism

is a symphony
The German cares for a dancing baby goat
The pirates laugh
A finch bathes in two cupped hands

California Burgers and loaded potatoes
Anyone know if the road to the falls is open?
Transvaginal mesh complaint department now open
Stow away with me
For a hundred days in Europe
A cat mugshot: "but it was medical catnip!"
Us meercats can't stay awake in class and look ridiculous
Back again, in Anaheim. "Waitress I need two more boat drinks!"
California spend more on prison then education.

Looking for treasure in a draught low lake.

A shared quest:
Pacifica and the Earth Charter.
Fracking has used 250 billion gallons of fresh water since 2005
The cat is thirsty

WORDS ARE DEVILED EGGS

Last night I dreamed of witches battling
on suburban lawns.
I stuck with it, holding my ground,
even when the security forces
retired for the evening.
I am not sure who won
but I had a pen as a wand
and I am still here.

This mourning, I wake
a little more fully thinking about the magic
of life sentences and hating words
amidst the great love affair I've been having
with them. Lockhart says "Words are Eggs.".
Does he know it's possible to over-boil?
Some are too soft, too yokey,
too rotten for anyone to consume other
than Vulture or Raccoon.

Some are so creamy and tangy
the angels in heaven
sing on your tongue.

But words are bridges of pencil sticks
not holy gates;
They can be tombs, uteruses, time capsules, socks.

Sometimes syllables are rocks on a watery path:
you don't know how deep you are in until you
step on one, and it turns out to be a turtle's back.
You sink in over your head
and even your camera around your neck
gets wet with humiliation
or whale's bile
like mine did, on my way to the Eagle's
nest.
Words give birth
but their talons carry away:
their beaks murder what is underneath.
just when I think they are bringing me closer
I look behind me
and see they are taking me further away;
just when I think I am revealing,
I see my letters are only another layer.

(Reprinted from Immanence: The Journal of Applied Myth, Story and Folklore, Volume 1, 2015)

CAPTAIN KIRK DREAM

I am part of a large group or organization, moving forward down the hallway with the crowd.

Captain Kirk from Star Trek is facing me. He is smiling, looking into my eyes,
Connecting, acknowledging me warmly and lovingly.

We are walking towards the door; we are all going to go on a special trip:
There will be important work done and fancy dinners with dignitaries.

At the door, Captain Kirk and I are becoming aware I am bear-footed.
The air seems to shimmer. Self-awareness of my naked feet
is feeling good and free and natural.
Captain Kirk is smiling fondly and accepting me as I am;
I am smiling sheepishly

I am accepting myself as I am and at same time wanting to honor the accepted customs of those we are going to meet in the future.

I am asking for a few minutes to go back and collect my shoes and prepare for our outing.
I am planning to run back to the door shortly.

In my bed room, the closest is so full and disorganized, but
I am seeing my favorite "Fiesta" flower dress sitting out on the jewelry box.
The strap had come undone, but I grab the dress and the beautiful, Alaskan Native sewing kit
(the one with golden scissors the shape of Snake, or is it Heron?)
My grandmotherly friend Dorothy made this for me: she is an elder who is on the Board of the Federation of Alaskan Natives,
and Aunt of Valerie, the girl who went missing in the woods, forever.
She gifted me the sewing kit for helping the family make a website

and for talking with the Christian in her clan, who want to re-member

the old, indigenous ways of knowing.

I am rushing outside... I don't want the others to have to wait for me, but a few minutes.
My classmates, along with Captain Kirk have come to fetch me....
They have the backs open of several large vehicles and many are encouraging me to jump in:
I am feeling grateful for so many sets of welcoming people to ride with:
I am feeling blessed my colleagues/friends came for me.
I am diving into the closest vehicle.

We are all sensing urgency in the air:
Even though we are feeling excitement and friendship and love,
the world outside that we are going out to be meeting and helping
is dark and full of turmoil.

WHEN HERONS MOVE AS ONE

When Herons move as One
shimmering body of white amidst the teal
sea of sky
forms take shape in some archaic language of
whales
and angels who bow their heads
like the bow of violin on spiders' strings.
 This is when crickets making love
in the desert leaves
us breathless like autumn's empty branches
and I fall away to nothingness
and become an empty reed.

This is when I hear my voice
and understand the weight
of my own authority
the ground I stand on,
the granite that flows.
This is when I close my eyes and see through years
and ages
and feel the push and pull of our flock-bodies migrating

back to our primordial nesting grounds.

When Herons move as One
we harmonize as wisps of wind;

molecules which hold and lift the weighty avian
beak and bone and claw.
When we can dig in to this song-line
I am you and you are me and we are us!
Aloneness recedes deep underground.
This is when we fly and move as Mercury,
as hot lava at Mt. Vesuvius covering the dead
as Eros and Psyche's love reunited
after all of Aphrodite's impossible tests—
perched, now, on the lap of a golden
thrown of feathers
high on Mt. Olympus.

When Herons move as One, God
breathes and we become the pause
between the inhale and the sigh;
we become the lift between
the current and the mighty wing.
the sun shines through the clouds that frame

this dream of flight;
This is destiny's movement.
Only then do we become safe landing
guiding all at once to the light.

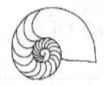

PHOTOSYNTHESIS: A LOVE STORY, PART 1

"I wish I could see you before I leave..."
she said to him, sadly.

"He looked at her, smiled kindly and inquired,
are you a tree? And if so, what season are you in,
fall, or spring?"

And she said to him, "When you are far away
my limbs shiver and my strength goes underground,
so it is winter.

But when you are near me, I
 blossom into the fullness
of my being, and it is always summertime."

And he replied, "My darling, do not fret. For I am the sun.
Whether your limbs are bare, or lush with green
I will be with you, on the morrow
and as long as your roots are anchored in the earth.

Then, she waved her branches at him, three times

and blew him a kiss on the wings of a cardinal that
flew towards him,
as he bathed her in his glorious light,
stroking her bark with his rays,
warming her until her buds opened for him.

They made love in
photosynthesis."

PHOTOSYNTHESIS: A LOVE STORY, PART 2

"Are you jealous that I love other celestial bodies, too?"
She asked her favorite lover, the Sun.
"Are you jealous that I love other foliage?" He replied to the tree.
"Sometimes, Yes. But I know that each Elm and Oak, each Pecan and Almond, are unique
and you have enough heat for all of us."
"It is true", he agreed. "But do you also know that your own special verdancy makes me shine in ways no other deciduous tree can do? You dance rings around the others."
That made her smile. But it wasn't enough.
"What about the conifers? Do you prefer them, because they never take leaves of you; they never show their bark, as I do? Because they pine for you, too?"
"No. I love you most of all, because you bare your trunk in winter;
in Spring your new leaves quake and quiver,
you light on fire, and become my mirror: crimson and gold to draw me back to you each autumn,
and then you sway with me, all summer long."

"Will you hug me?" She asked him, and continued,
"I won't speak to you. I'll just hug back. I promise.
Can we just have a moment to breath deeply together?"
He smiled at her and said,
"If you stand very still, at the golden hour,
you will feel my warmth, like no other."

ANGELS ON THE SAND ASCENDING

She wept in his arms as he kissed her,
finally, finally.

And the taste of the salt of her tears brought him to
the shores of an ancient ocean,
and the warm honey of her mouth dropped him into
fields of golden wildflowers; into the desire of bees.
Where he had only known darkness and death before,
Now he knew green. "So this is what they meant when
they spoke of "Summer"". He wept softly like the
August rains and kissed his bride-queen with all the
passion of the season.

Her body trembled and quaked under the quelling of
his July hands,
and her movement, which he felt like sunflowers
stretching in every cell of his being, gave rise to
trees.

His blood began rushing through his veins — a flash
flood moving through a red rock canyon;

his heart burst open like the conical seeds of Black
Spruce;
he became at once forest fire and hearth fire.

It was no longer enough to fill her with his ideas,
or his tongue, or to run his hands over the peeks and
vales of her. Her quiet sobs of grief; of gratitude and
release were turning to moans of other things.

He thought he could almost hear African Elephants
calling to their mates across the vast savannah plains.
He could feel the Howler Monkeys sway from
branch-to-branch across the canopy-bed of clouds,
as they called and responded to the thunder gods, as
they knocked the promised fruits of the Citrons
down to him.
He had never been this close to her before,
yet he was fluent in the language of her body.
Her undulations were Braille, her sighs permissions.
He knew she was losing all sense of herself;
shapeshifting into something primal and animal.

He knew she was ready to receive him.
He felt at once like he was King of the Forest,
and slave to her.
And he was.

When he entered her, she gasped as pain met pleasure, and held her breath for a long moment. A blackbird flew to a higher branch; A deer held her ears back, and twitched them.
She knew that if she surrendered to him, she would be lost to her old life: she would be lost to anything and everyone but him. She told herself to resist him, to fight desire, to pull away.
For a moment, she did.
But even that movement of retreat was felt as intensely as anything
they had ever done to each other, and it excited them both.
How could she resist him?
That would be a denial of her own soul.
With that carnal knowledge, she surrendered to him, completely:
she relinquished her will to her deepest Self.
As he filled the vessel of her body with his,

she became Blue Flame. Then, mountain air. Then,
water.
He moved in her slowly, rhythmically, as a boatman
dips his oars into the rippling of a lake.

They rowed this way together across time, across
space,
out into the deepest recesses of the river,
until they became one oar, one vessel, one ripple
and finally,
the blackness underneath.

Then, they disappeared, completely.

At that very moment, a chickadee was eating seeds
out of an old, grinning woman's hands.
On the other side of the island, a whale breached,
and a seal splashed.
A giant flock of Blue Herons performed aerials in the
sky, in unison
to delight the Angels who were sunbathing
on the sand.

Hades smiled, underneath, at his living dream.

MY MIRROR

I love how the water reflects the sunlight and the trees and even the moon when it is inky black, and how babies giggle whenever their mothers smile at them and sons visually fill with pride, with contentment when heir fathers nod their heads as if to say, "Good Job."
I love how I can ramble on for pages and pages straight
or post a dozen things all at once until it seems nothing but chaos, and you will still go right to the essence of it all
finding the diamond of me within my pile
of coal.I love how no matter how cold I am toward you
you reflect the sun's heat and warm my heart with your attention and grace. You are like my twin, but even better,
because you don't yell at me, or steal my clothes
— though I'd give you the shirt off my back
If you would just hold me close.
But mirrors don't have hands, do they? Not unless they are my own.

Would I be Narcissus if I dove into the reflection of
myself
to find and kiss you?
I'd be willing to drown
to find out.

QUESTIONS IN THE FOREST

This is what I do not understand:

Why we cannot be as open about who we are
as the Cottonwood is about her seeds;
Why that wooly abundance that gives fragrance to
the Balm of Gilead
is not part of our own release
in the Spring time of our loving?

This is what I can not fathom
when I gaze into the well and watch the tadpole
treading;
why in the youth of our old age
we are not leaping for everything
God is offering us:
the dragon fly so easily caught with the curl of our
toad tongue;
the view from the top of trees
the golden ball a Princess dropped in the ravine.
She waits, you know, for the Frog Prince's bargain,
even though he will traipse mud across the ballroom
floor of her reckoning

and sit at the table of her awakening.
For you see she knows the end
of the story.

What I do not know
and wish I did is why you are not puckering your lips
and croaking at my door.
How you are settling for a sapling
when the whole forest
could be yours?

BLIND STAR

The very sad thing about stars
is I can see them but never seem
to be able to get close
enough to sparkle
Would I burn up if I did?
Or turn to ice?
Other people seem
to have no problem with this
but the earth is too dark for me
and it isn't enough that I can
glimpse one
I long for twinkling eyes to wonder too
at the sight of me.

If only I had been born a comet
or understood the will
of the Milky Way
I must be drinking
too much gravity
For I hiccup moonbeams
but no one sees or
comments

MY BODY IS BRAILLE

My body is Braille
on the white page of glacier
The swirl of a Zephyr's fingerprints
whirlpool around vowels of ears and nose
and slip under open jacket
seeking secrets from the still
smoldering campfire
under neath bed clothes hinting
accentual verse.

A gluttonous gale slaps rosy
cheeks, sentencing
skin to paragraphs only fit
for penguins and polar bears.

Our fate is written on Time's breath-carved
rock face neither smiling nor smirking
but constellating such quiet
consternation in its frozen
countenance that the queen's sentry
or librarian
would be proud.

A King Eider leaves a wake
in the azure of moraine lake a single tear
calves
into the water,
causing tidal wave
to a Neptune Snail
as I sigh your name.

Look as my breath freezes a perfect
"O" floating in the air of time
Vapors evaporate and nigh
enigmatically falling on to the acrostic
pebbled
ground.
Some break.
Some bounce.
With you I am glacier
but also warm
breeze
and the ball at the bottom
of a sing-a-long.

MEET THE AUTHOR

Amy Beth Katz, M.A. is a poet, dream-shaman, soul guide, Jungian/depth practitioner, photographer, clairvoyant, cross-cultural communication specialist, wilderness rite of passage guide, teacher and keynote speaker. She has authored numerous books of poetry and personal growth, including The Lizard Thieves: Love Poems Amy has been engaging in a radical experiment: cultivating her obsessions with her soul's calling. This includes the pursuit of unconditional love, intentional synchronicity, expanded awareness and healing through the intuitive and creative arts, unity consciousness, and the emergent interplay of dreams and material imagination.
Learn more about Amy Beth Katz by visiting:

www.schooloflivingdreams.com

Farewell, farewell! but this I tell
To thee, thou Wedding-Guest!
He prayeth well, who loveth well
Both man and bird and beast.

He prayeth best, who loveth best
All things both great and small;
For the dear God who loveth us,
He made and loveth all.

The Mariner, whose eye is bright,
Whose beard with age is hoar,
Is gone: and now the Wedding-Guest
Turned from the bridegroom's door.

He went like one that hath been stunned,
And is of sense forlorn:
A sadder and a wiser man,
He rose the morrow morn.

— Samuel Taylor Coleridge, "Rime of the Ancient Mariner"

www.ingramcontent.com/pod-product-compliance
Lightning Source LLC
LaVergne TN
LVHW020935090426
835512LV00020B/3362